Contents

INTRODUCTION. 2

What is Noom? 3

What is the Noom diet? 4

    How does the Noom diet work? 6

    How do you get started and how much does Noom cost? 7

    Is there any evidence for its effectiveness? 9

Research into the Noom app 10

    Why could the Noom diet work for you? 12

Benefits of Noom 14

Is Noom a heart-healthy diet? 26

Recipies for the Noom Diet 29

INTRODUCTION.

The secret to losing body weight and keeping it off for good? Creating healthy habits you actually enjoy and can stick to consistently. Easier said than done, of course. Noom is the latest company that wants to change that. The weight loss app and personalized meal-planning service blew up as the third most Googled diet last year. With more than 45 million dedicated users worldwide, the Noom app aims to help people create sustainable habits so they can lose weight at a realistic pace and maintain a healthy lifestyle for the long haul.

Noom users say it's helping them finally reach their health and weight-loss goals. "I am moving more and making better food choices...I feel like I am erasing 30+ years of bad habits a little each day," wrote one user. Another, who claimed she lost 50 pounds over one year on the plan, said, "Noom helped me work through so many of my life issues where I was stuck! I hit my goal and kept going. I felt like the pace was perfect." Not every review is as stellar, though—scroll through the user reviews and you'll find several complaints about technical issues, communication with coaches, and pricing.

What is Noom?

Noom is a mobile app you can download to your smartphone or tablet. By focusing on behavioral changes, Noom calls itself a lifestyle, not a diet.

The app provides:

Weekly challenges and educational information. Topics involve nutrition, stress management, goal setting, and healthy habit formation.

Tools to track your progress. These allow you to log your meals, exercise regimen, and body weight.

A virtual coaching team. A goal specialist, group coach, and support group are meant to help you stay on track.

Biometric tracking. These features help you monitor blood sugar and blood pressure.

Noom allows you to log exercise, weight loss over time, and blood sugar levels as well as blood pressure. The diet itself begins after you take an in-depth quiz based on a series of lifestyle questions — calorie restrictions are recommended on a case by case basis, and they may recommend a diabetes management plan. Unlike the weight loss plan, the diabetes Noom plan is designed to particularly aid individuals suffering from both type 1 and type 2 diabetes, and may help prevent overweight or obese individuals from becoming pre-diabetic (it's even recognized by the Centers for Disease Control and Prevention).

What is the Noom diet?

For starters, for anyone who is TOTALLY new to it, Noom is a smartphone app used to help you change your dietary habits and therefore lose weight. You start by taking their short online quiz during which you'll answer questions about your weight-loss goals and preferred coaching style. The Noom quiz also gives you your expected weight loss schedule.

The Noom app allows people to self-monitor their weight loss. Noom is an app designed to help people lose weight, get fit, and stay healthy. It uses a unique traffic light system to rank foods according to how many calories they contain. "Green" foods, such as spinach and broccoli, are the least calorie dense, whereas "red" foods contain more calories and should make up less of a portion.

Using these data, the app's creators develop personalized weight loss plans that they claim can help deliver long lasting weight loss results. To get a personalized weight loss plan, a person will need to purchase a subscription and answer some questions on the Noom website or app. The algorithm will then design a weight loss plan to fit the person's needs. Shortly after a person logs in for the first time, the app will pair them with an appropriate health coach. The coach will provide relevant dietary information and advice to help the person achieve their weight goals.

Noom also includes a daily calorie target, which adjusts based on how much activity you got that day (you manually log your exercise or sync up to your Fitbit or Apple Watch). One of my favorite features of Noom is the comprehensive food log where you type in what you ate and track your daily calories. If your food isn't in Noom's database, you can manually add the nutrition information. It also provides a color-coded breakdown of your food based on how calorie-dense they are: green (fruits, veggies, most whole grains, complex carbs), yellow (lean meats, starches, eggs), and red (typically processed junk food but also healthy calorie-dense foods like oils and nuts). You are supposed to aim to eat as many green and yellow foods as possible and limit your red foods to 25 percent or less of your diet.

Here is a quick overview of the Noom Diet Plan, followed by some examples of a day in the life of a Noomer.

- No foods are off-limits.

- Foods are all classified using a red-yellow-green food system. Like a traffic light.

- Nutrient-dense foods are encouraged, they are your green foods.

- Proteins and starches are limited, they are yellow.

Foods higher in fat and empty calories, especially things like pizza, candy, alcohol are red. While pretty limited, red foods are part of your allotment every day! You are just learning to balance them and eat them in moderation.

How does the Noom diet work?
Before you sign up, you have to answer some simple questions about your weight and how much you want to lose, and then the computer's algorithm will work out your weight loss goal and a weekly plan on how to achieve it.

"Essentially, Noom combines a calorie budget alongside information on which foods you should aim to eat more of, and which to eat less of," explains Dr Gall. "Noom's plans are non-restrictive, meaning that no foods are off limits, but it works to reinforce healthy eating habits by using a traffic light system."

The app even offers access to a "health coach". So, you can ask direct questions (such as what to pick for dinner in a restaurant) when you're feeling stuck.

Noom aims to help you lose weight like most commercial diet plans and programs — by creating a calorie deficit. A calorie deficit occurs when you consistently consume fewer calories than you burn each day. Noom estimates your daily calorie needs based on your gender, age, height, weight, and your answers to a series of lifestyle questions. Depending on your goal weight and timeframe, Noom uses an algorithm to estimate how many calories you need to eat each day. This is known as your calorie budget.

For safety reasons and to ensure adequate nutrition, the app does not allow a daily calorie budget below 1,200 calories for women or 1,400 calories for men. Noom encourages food logging and daily weigh-ins — two self-monitoring behaviors associated with weight loss and long-term weight loss maintenance.

How do you get started and how much does Noom cost?

The Noom app itself is free to download or you can start the process on their website. You'll first be taken through a detailed quiz that has three parts; first, you'll go through the demographic profile section that asks for your height and weight, as well as what your health goals are and if you have a goal weight in mind. After answering some preliminary lifestyle questions and information about your current health status or conditions, you input your email address and a program plan is revealed estimating how much time it will take you to lose the desired amount of weight.

The second part of the quiz looks at habits and behaviors, and allows you to pick a focus for your plan on nutrition, physical activity, or building good habits. Finally, the activity and nutrition portion includes basic questions about your current health practices as well as behavior change questions. After this step, to claim your personalized plan Noom requires a credit card.

Noom is currently offering a 7-day trial option for as little as $0.50 on their website given the current global health crisis, but after that your card will be charged to continue. Program pricing starts out at $59/month, but the price goes down as you commit to longer periods of time. The cheapest price you can get Noom for is on their annual auto-recurring plan which costs $199 (averages to just over $16 a month). And if you refer a friend, they'll get a 20% discount and you'll receive a $20 Amazon credit as well.

Is there any evidence for its effectiveness?

Apps such as Noom encourage people to self-monitor their weight loss on a regular basis. A 2017 study found that people who frequently and consistently record their dietary habits experience more consistent and long-term weight loss.

However, self-monitoring weight loss is a practice that tends to decrease quickly over time. To prevent this, the Noom app provides features to motivate people to continue self-monitoring.

These features include access to both a health coach and a social platform where people can discuss their weight loss challenges and successes with other users.

Noom's strong points are its sensible approach to nutrition and straightforward logging. You don't need an app to do that. A calculator and paper notebook would suffice. But Noom makes it a lot easier. Seeing the weight graph trend downwards is rewarding, and having an easy-to-use interface to log your meals is great for keeping track of your intake.

I also really appreciated how private Noom let me be during this process. There were no forbidden foods, so I didn't have to explain to anyone that I was on a special diet when I dined with them. When we were done with our meals, I just typed a few things on my phone and that was it. There were no meetings to attend, so I didn't have to worry about coordinating my schedule with whatever meetings were available. I could read—or ignore—the content they provided at the time that was most convenient for me, whether that was on the subway, in line at CVS, or in my kitchen making a meal. My outward behavior didn't change, beyond preparing more meals at home instead of eating takeout lunches. (No one in the office even knew I was testing Noom, aside from my editor.) In essence, I feel like I lost 20 pounds in 100 days just by staring at my phone.

Weight loss apps are a lot like dating apps: The most successful customers are also the ones who ultimately no longer need it. The difference, of course, is that instead of ending up in a relationship with another person, Noom forces you to work hard on establishing a better (and hopefully long-term) relationship with food, and with yourself.

Research into the Noom app

In 2016, some researchers conducted a study of the effectiveness of the Noom app. The study analyzed dietary data from Noom users who recorded what they ate at least twice a month for 6 months.

Of 35,921 Noom users, 77.9% reported a reduction in body weight while using the app. The researchers found that users who monitored their weight and dietary habits more frequently experienced more consistent weight loss.

In a separate study, also from 2016, researchers used Noom to deliver a diabetes prevention program (DPP) to 43 participants with prediabetes. At the start of the study, each participant had either overweight or obesity. The purpose of the study was to investigate the efficacy of the DPP in promoting weight loss among the participants.

The participants had experienced significant weight loss by week 16 and week 24 of using the DPP. Of the 36 participants who completed the study, 64% lost more than 5% of their body weight.

However, the study did not compare the Noom diet with any other app or diet. It is, therefore, difficult to know whether the Noom diet is any more effective than other weight loss strategies.

Why could the Noom diet work for you?

Seeing as most of us carry our phones everywhere, it's easy to track what you're eating. In fact, you'll probably only need to spend around 5-10 minutes a day on the app filling in your progress. Forgotten to add something in? Your health coach will prompt you to help you stay on track.

"Keeping a food diary can be incredibly helpful if you're trying to lose weight," says Dr Gall. "Being able to see what you're eating on a daily basis can help you to identify positive and negative eating habits, and can make you more aware of the calories that you consume. You may even be less likely to snack on foods with a high-calorie density as you'll know that you need to record it, so you might opt for healthier snacks instead."

And looking at the #NoomNerds hashtag on social media, results have been impressive, with a study claiming that out of 36,000 Noom users, 77.9 per cent reported weight loss.

Is it worth a try?

If you have the money to spare and like a trend, then give it a go. But it's not your only option if money is tight at this time of year.

"There are free options available," says Dr Gall. "If you're struggling on your own, you can always make an appointment to see your doctor to discuss your concerns and difficulties. You may be referred to a nutritionist or dietician for advice. You can still create a record of your eating habits by using free apps, or just by writing your meals and snacks in a diary. The advantage to this is that you may have regular appointments to check your progress, so your doctor can intervene if they think there could be a problem."

One of the benefits users of the Noom app seem to universally rate is the group chats they can join in with. Which is no wonder, seeing as new research by WW found a third of people think they will give up their diet sooner without someone to support them along their journey.

"Online communities are fantastic for people that are wanting to lose weight, as you're all there to achieve the same goal. They're a great place to share tips and motivational stories, as well as having somewhere to vent if you're struggling to people that understand what you're going through," says Dr Gall.

Benefits of Noom

Noom's program emphasizes a long-term approach to weight loss. It may have several benefits over quick-fix methods.

Focuses on calorie and nutrient density

Noom emphasizes calorie density, a measure of how many calories a food or beverage provides relative to its weight or volume. The program categorizes foods into a color system — green, yellow, and red — based on their calorie density and concentration of nutrients.

Foods with the lowest calorie density, highest concentration of nutrients, or both, are considered green. Foods with the highest calorie density, lowest concentration of nutrients, or both, are labeled red, while yellow foods fall in between.

Calorie-dense foods contain a large number of calories in a small amount of food, whereas items of low calorie density have fewer calories in a large amount of food.

Generally, low-calorie-dense foods, such as fruits and vegetables, contain more water and fiber and are low in fat. On the other hand, high-calorie-dense foods, such as fatty fish, meats, nut butters, sweets, and desserts, typically provide fat or added sugars but lack water and fiber.

Diets comprised mainly of low-calorie-dense foods and beverages are associated with less hunger, weight loss, and risk of chronic conditions like heart disease than diets rich in high-calorie-dense foods.

No food is off limits

Several popular diets can be restricting by limiting certain foods or entire food groups. This can promote disordered eating or obsessive behaviors surrounding healthy or "clean" eating. Noom takes the opposite approach, offering flexibility by allowing all foods to fit into your diet. Because some high-calorie-dense foods like nuts contain important nutrients, and completely eliminating desserts and other treats is neither realistic nor worthwhile, Noom doesn't forbid these items but encourages less of them.

The program does this to help you stay within or near your daily calorie budget. Noom's library of recipes also helps you determine which foods and recipes are appropriate for you based on any food allergies or intolerances you may have.

Promotes behavioral changes

Losing weight and leading a healthy lifestyle goes beyond what and how much you eat. It's also about forming new healthy behaviors, reinforcing the healthy habits you already have, and breaking any unhealthy patterns that sabotage your goals.

Without behavioral change, any weight lost with a reduced-calorie diet tends to be regained over time — often in excess of what was initially lost. In fact, in a review of 29 long-term weight loss studies, people gained back 33% of their initial weight loss at 1 year, on average, and 79% after 5 years .

Recognizing that behavioral change is difficult, Noom uses a psychology-based curriculum that encourages self-efficacy — the belief in your ability to execute habits necessary to reach your goals.

In this way, Noom may better equip you with the tools and education necessary for effective behavioral change that underlies successful long-term weight loss maintenance. Indeed, one study found that 78% of nearly 36,000 Noom users sustained their weight loss over 9 months. It's unclear whether weight loss is sustained after this time

It's scientifically validated

Noom has been scientifically studied (although minimally) and shown to help people lose weight and keep it off. In one study among almost 36,000 people who were Noom users, almost 80 percent reported weight loss while using the app for a median of 267 days. Among the group, certain behaviors promoted better results: Tracking dinner was an especially effective strategy, while tracking overall calories, activity and weight weren't far behind.

A second, much (much!) smaller study among just 43 overweight and obese Noom participants found that the plan led to a 5 percent loss of body weight — an amount that sounds small, but it's been tied to really meaningful health improvements. Again, weekly weigh ins and meals logged were the main predictors of success.

The Cons

Several red flags jump out at me. Here are some to keep in mind.

The food categories are flawed

I'm all for encouraging fruit and veggie consumption, but the calorie density approach doesn't take into account how filling, delicious and healthful many high-calorie dense foods are. Nuts, seeds, olives and avocados — along with their butters and oils — all supply protective plant compounds that help lower the inflammatory process, thereby lowering your risk of disease. These same foods as part of a healthful eating pattern have also been linked with improvements in body weight and waist measurements, and they may make it easier to prevent weight gain, which is a huge step toward aging healthfully.

And in my experience, people enjoy the green-light foods so much more when they're served with these plant-based fats. Wouldn't you rather have a salad with some crunch from nuts, creaminess from avocado, and a delicious dressing made with extra virgin olive oil compared to a salad with crunch from carrots and a sparse dressing? Granted, you can have either with Noom, but putting healthful fats in the red zone is misleading and may lead you to unnecessarily restrict them.

Reviews online are mixed

Many people complain that the coaching is inconsistent (and some say practically non-existent) and that the responses feel canned. People also complain that the database lacks many foods, is unreliable, and that tracking food on this plan is a big pain. That's a big drawback given that tracking is integral to this program's success (according to the research). There are also a notable number of complaints about canceling the program.

Health coaches don't have the same qualifications as registered dietitians

I don't like to knock any program or plan that makes people feel mentally and physically healthier. However, I will point out that there's a huge difference in education and training between a health coach and an RD. If you have any food sensitivities, medical concerns, or other roadblocks to eating better (including lifestyle issues, like business travel or inexperience cooking), you'd be better off working one on one with someone who can help you discover what works best for your unique body and circumstances.

On top of that, based on reviews, the health coaching is really over billed. Among the common complaints: people felt like they were talking to a chat bot instead of a person; the coaching support is superficial; coaches aren't available 24/7 and often leave you hanging.

When I tried the app, I asked a few questions and felt like responses were slow and vague. For example, on day one I asked, "How come I can't find my food log?" and on day two, I got a response that said, "As we begin the journey, I want to point out one opportunity to get closer to your Super Goal: meal logging!" There was no further explanation on how to find the food log, which I eventually found on my own.

Calories might dip too low

In one online review, a reviewer said the app recommended an 1,100 calorie diet. This is too low to get all of the nutrients you need to thrive. Though the reviewer said she got used to this calorie level, most people would find this amount to be severely restrictive and limiting and I would never advise anyone to eat this few calories. In my case, the app suggested 1,200 calories, which is also too low.

While tracking can be an effective tool, studies also indicate that you don't need to count calories if you stick to a few basic principles: Eat more whole foods, eat more veggies, and eat fewer processed foods and sugary foods.

Foods to eat and avoid

Noom categorizes food as green, yellow, or red based on its calorie and nutrient density. The app recommends consuming a set percentage of foods from each color — 30% green, 45% yellow, and 25% red.

According to the Noom website, these are examples of foods for each color (26):

Green

- Fruits: bananas, apples, strawberries, watermelon, blueberries

- Vegetables: tomatoes, cucumbers, salad greens, carrots, onions, spinach

- Starchy vegetables: parsnips, beets, sweet potatoes, squash

- Diary: skim milk, non-fat yogurt, non-fat Greek yogurt, non-fat cheese sticks

- Dairy alternatives: unsweetened almond, cashew, or soy milk

- Whole grains: oatmeal, brown rice, whole-grain bread, whole-grain pita, whole-grain pasta, whole-grain tortilla, whole-grain cereals

- Condiments: marinara, salsa, sauerkraut, ketchup, light mayo

- Beverages: unsweetened tea and coffee

Yellow

- Lean meats: grilled chicken, turkey, and lean cuts of beef, pork, and lamb

- Seafood: tuna, salmon, tilapia, scallops

- Dairy: low-fat milk, low-fat cheeses, low-fat cottage cheese, Greek yogurt

- Legumes and seeds: lentils, pinto beans, chickpeas, peas, quinoa, black beans, soy beans

- Grains and grain products: couscous, white rice, white bread, white pasta

- Beverages: diet soda, beer

Red

- Meats: ham, red meats, fried meats, bacon, sausage, hot dogs, hamburgers

- Nuts and nut butters: peanut butter, almond butter, almonds, walnuts

- Desserts and sweets: cake, chocolate, cookies, candy, pastries

- Snack foods: french fries, potato chips, energy and snack bars

- Condiments and toppings: butter, mayonnaise, ranch dressing

- Beverages: wine, juices like orange juice

One-week sample menu

Below is 1-week sample meal plan using recipes from Noom's app.

This meal plan would not apply to everyone since calorie recommendations are individualized, but it provides a general overview of the foods included from the green, yellow, and red categories.

Monday

Breakfast: raspberry yogurt parfait

Lunch: vegetarian barley soup

Dinner: fennel, orange, and arugula salad

Snack: creamy cucumber and dill salad

Tuesday

Breakfast: banana-ginger smoothie

Lunch: roasted orange tilapia and asparagus

Dinner: mushroom and rice soup

Snack: deviled eggs

Wednesday

Breakfast: vegetable skillet frittata

Lunch: broccoli quinoa pilaf

Dinner: pork lettuce wraps

Snack: homemade yogurt pops

Thursday

Breakfast: egg sandwich

Lunch: chicken and avocado pita pockets

Dinner: pasta with shellfish and mushrooms

Snack: mixed nuts

Friday

Breakfast: spinach-tomato frittata

Lunch: salmon with tabbouleh salad

Dinner: grilled chicken with corn salsa

Snack: chocolate cake

Saturday

Breakfast: banana-apple and nut oatmeal

Lunch: turkey cheddar tacos

Dinner: green bean casserole

Snack: hummus and peppers

Sunday

Breakfast: scrambled egg wrap

Lunch: loaded spinach salad

Dinner: salmon patties with green beans

Snack: cream cheese fruit dip with apples

Possible risks

A limitation of the Noom app is that it does not allow the user to record information on nutrients other than calories. However, a healthful diet should contain a good amount of micronutrients, such as vitamins and minerals. As a result of this limitation, people using the Noom app will have incomplete information on the healthfulness of their food choices. It also means that doctors and dietitians may be reluctant to recommend the app.

Additionally, some Noom coaches do not have certification from the National Board for Health & Wellness Coaching. This certification requires a coach to meet the minimum standard of knowledge and skills necessary for health and wellness coaching.

Coaches without this certification could potentially offer inappropriate advice. Also, people who have a complicated medical history should take extra care when using Noom or similar weight loss apps. These individuals should seek additional weight loss advice from a doctor, dietitian, or other healthcare professional.

Is Noom a heart-healthy diet?
Yes, Noom is largely compatible with recommendations for a heart-healthy diet from nutritionists and the medical community. An eating pattern that encourages

veggies, fruits and whole grains but is light on saturated fats and salt is considered the best way to keep cholesterol and blood pressure in check. However, the plan does not directly address salt reduction. You can track blood pressure readings on the app.

A study published in May 2016 in the Journal of Research in Medical Sciences looked at the effect of a low-calorie-dense diet on reducing cardiovascular risks following recent weight loss. Among 70 participants, those on the low-calorie diet reduced their blood levels of total cholesterol and (bad) LDL cholesterol.

Can Noom prevent or control diabetes?

It's possible that Noom may help prevent or control diabetes. Being obese or overweight is a risk factor for Type 2 diabetes and losing weight can lower your risk. Following a balanced diet low in sugary foods can reduce your long-term blood glucose levels.

Noom is included in the national registry of recognized diabetes prevention programs, which is compiled by the Centers for Disease Control and Prevention.

Prevention:

In a large, long-term observation study following more than 143,000 women for about 12 years, published in

2017 in the Journal of the Academy of Nutrition and Dietetics, the risk of developing Type 2 diabetes was 24% higher for women who ate diets higher in calorie density compared to women who followed a low-energy-density diet.

A study published in 2007 in the journal Diabetes Care found that adults on a low-calorie-dense diet had lower fasting insulin levels than those on diets with more high-calorie-dense foods. According to the authors, low-calorie dense diets help prevent insulin resistance, which is a common precursor to Type 2 diabetes.

Control: A lower-calorie-density diet was associated with a healthy dietary pattern for patients with Type 2 diabetes in a study of about 1,600 Japanese patients attending diabetes clinics, in an article published in the June 2019 issue of Diabetes.

Does Noom allow for restrictions and preferences?

Most people can customize Noom to fit their needs, since there are no taboo foods.

Supplement recommended? Noom does not promote supplement use.

Vegetarian and vegan: Noom is doable whether you're looking for a vegetarian or vegan plan. Low-caloric density, high-water foods favored by Noom – such as fruits, veggies and whole grains – fit perfectly into a vegan or vegetarian eating style. See all plant-based diets »

Gluten-free: You're free to choose gluten-free foods as part of your Noom daily calorie budget. See all gluten-free diets »

Low-salt: Low-salt foods are fine if you follow Noom. However, it's up to you to track down specific low-salt or no-salt items and tally your own daily sodium totals. See all low-salt diets »

Kosher: It's possible to keep Kosher with Noom – you simply fill in those foods when your log your daily meals. However, the Noom app does not offer specifically designated Kosher recipes. See all kosher diets »

Halal: Noom does not offer any specifically designated halal recipes

Recipies for the Noom Diet

Taco Seasoning I

Recipe Summary

prep: 1 min

total: 1 min

Servings: 10

Yield: 1 ounce

Ingredients

- 1 tablespoon chili powder
- ¼ teaspoon garlic powder
- ¼ teaspoon onion powder
- ¼ teaspoon crushed red pepper flakes
- ¼ teaspoon dried oregano
- ½ teaspoon paprika
- 1 ½ teaspoons ground cumin
- 1 teaspoon sea salt
- 1 teaspoon black pepper

Directions

Instructions

Step 1

In a small bowl, mix together chili powder, garlic powder, onion powder, red pepper flakes, oregano, paprika, cumin, salt and pepper. Store in an airtight container.

Nutrition Facts

Per Serving:

5 calories; protein 0.2g; carbohydrates 0.9g; fat 0.2g; cholesterol 0mg; sodium 184.8mg 7% DV.

Guacamole

Recipe Summary

prep: 10 mins

total: 10 mins

Servings: 4

Yield: 4 servings

Ingredients

- 3 avocados - peeled, pitted, and mashed
- 1 lime, juiced
- 1 teaspoon salt
- ½ cup diced onion
- 3 tablespoons chopped fresh cilantro
- 2 roma (plum) tomatoes, diced
- 1 teaspoon minced garlic
- 1 pinch ground cayenne pepper (Optional)

Directions

Instructions

Step 1

In a medium bowl, mash together the avocados, lime juice, and salt. Mix in onion, cilantro, tomatoes, and garlic. Stir in cayenne pepper. Refrigerate 1 hour for best flavor, or serve immediately.

Nutrition Facts

Per Serving:

262 calories; protein 3.7g 7% DV; carbohydrates 18g 6% DV; fat 22.2g 34% DV; cholesterol 0mg; sodium 595.7mg 24% DV.

Garlic Prime Rib

Recipe Summary

prep: 10 mins

cook: 1 hr 30 mins

total: 1 hr 40 mins

Servings: 15

Yield: 1 10-pound roast

Ingredients

1 (10 pound) prime rib roast

10 cloves garlic, minced

2 tablespoons olive oil

2 teaspoons salt

2 teaspoons ground black pepper

2 teaspoons dried thyme

Directions

Instructions Checklist

Step 1

Place the roast in a roasting pan with the fatty side up. In a small bowl, mix together the garlic, olive oil, salt, pepper and thyme. Spread the mixture over the fatty layer of the roast, and let the roast sit out until it is at room temperature, no longer than 1 hour.

Step 2

Preheat the oven to 500 degrees F (260 degrees C).

Step 3

Bake the roast for 20 minutes in the preheated oven, then reduce the temperature to 325 degrees F (165 degrees C), and continue roasting for an additional 60 to 75 minutes. The internal temperature of the roast should be at 135 degrees F (57 degrees C) for medium rare.

Step 4

Allow the roast to rest for 10 or 15 minutes before carving so the meat can retain its juices.

Nutrition Facts

Per Serving:

562 calories; protein 29.6g 59% DV; carbohydrates 1g; fat 48g 74% DV; cholesterol 112.7mg 38% DV; sodium 395.5mg 16% DV.

Spinach and Feta Pita Bake

Recipe Summary

prep: 10 mins

cook: 12 mins

total: 22 mins

Servings: 6

Yield: 6 servings

Ingredients

- 1 (6 ounce) tub sun-dried tomato pesto
- 6 (6 inch) whole wheat pita breads
- 2 roma (plum) tomatoes, chopped
- 1 bunch spinach, rinsed and chopped
- 4 fresh mushrooms, sliced
- ½ cup crumbled feta cheese
- 2 tablespoons grated Parmesan cheese
- 3 tablespoons olive oil
- ground black pepper to taste

Directions

Instructions

Step 1

Preheat the oven to 350 degrees F (175 degrees C).

Step 2

Spread tomato pesto onto one side of each pita bread and place them pesto-side up on a baking sheet. Top pitas with tomatoes, spinach, mushrooms, feta cheese, and Parmesan cheese; drizzle with olive oil and season with pepper.

Step 3

Bake in the preheated oven until pita breads are crisp, about 12 minutes. Cut pitas into quarters.

Nutrition Facts

Per Serving:

350 calories; protein 11.6g 23% DV; carbohydrates 41.6g 13% DV; fat 17.1g 26% DV; cholesterol 12.6mg 4% DV; sodium 587.1mg 24% DV.

Foolproof Rib Roast

Recipe Summary

prep: 5 mins

cook: 5 hrs

total: 5 hrs 5 mins

Servings: 6

Yield: 6 servings

Ingredients

　　1 (5 pound) standing beef rib roast

　　2 teaspoons salt

　　1 teaspoon ground black pepper

　　1 teaspoon garlic powder

Directions

Instructions

Step 1

Allow roast to stand at room temperature for at least 1 hour.

Step 2

Preheat the oven to 375 degrees F (190 degrees C). Combine the salt, pepper and garlic powder in a small cup. Place the roast on a rack in a roasting pan so that the fatty side is up and the rib side is on the bottom. Rub the seasoning onto the roast.

Step 3

Roast for 1 hour in the preheated oven. Turn the oven off and leave the roast inside. Do not open the door.

Leave it in there for 3 hours. 30 to 40 minutes before serving, turn the oven back on at 375 degrees F (190 degrees C) to reheat the roast. The internal temperature should be at least 145 degrees F (62 degrees C). Remove from the oven and let rest for 10 minutes before carving into servings.

Nutrition Facts

Per Serving:

576 calories; protein 37g 74% DV; carbohydrates 0.6g; fat 46.2g 71% DV; cholesterol 137.2mg 46% DV; sodium 879.6mg 35% DV.

Marinated Grilled Shrimp

Recipe Summary

prep: 15 mins

cook: 6 mins

additional: 34 mins

total: 55 mins

Servings: 6

Yield: 6 servings

Ingredients

3 cloves garlic, minced

⅓ cup olive oil

¼ cup tomato sauce

2 tablespoons red wine vinegar

2 tablespoons chopped fresh basil

½ teaspoon salt

¼ teaspoon cayenne pepper

2 pounds fresh shrimp, peeled and deveined

skewers

Directions

Instructions

Step 1

In a large bowl, stir together the garlic, olive oil, tomato sauce, and red wine vinegar. Season with basil, salt, and cayenne pepper. Add shrimp to the bowl, and stir until evenly coated. Cover, and refrigerate for 30 minutes to 1 hour, stirring once or twice.

Step 2

Preheat grill for medium heat. Thread shrimp onto skewers, piercing once near the tail and once near the head. Discard marinade.

Step 3

Lightly oil grill grate. Cook shrimp on preheated grill for 2 to 3 minutes per side, or until opaque.

Nutrition Facts

Per Serving:

273 calories; protein 31g 62% DV; carbohydrates 2.8g 1% DV; fat 14.7g 23% DV; cholesterol 230mg 77% DV; sodium 471.8mg 19% DV.

Rosemary Roasted Turkey

Recipe Summary

prep: 25 mins

cook: 4 hrs

additional: 20 mins

total: 4 hrs 45 mins

Servings: 16

Yield: 1 (12 pound) turkey

Ingredients

¾ cup olive oil

3 tablespoons minced garlic

2 tablespoons chopped fresh rosemary

1 tablespoon chopped fresh basil

1 tablespoon Italian seasoning

1 teaspoon ground black pepper

salt to taste

1 (12 pound) whole turkey

Directions

Instructions

Step 1

Preheat oven to 325 degrees F (165 degrees C).

Step 2

In a small bowl, mix the olive oil, garlic, rosemary, basil, Italian seasoning, black pepper and salt. Set aside.

Step 3

Wash the turkey inside and out; pat dry. Remove any large fat deposits. Loosen the skin from the breast. This is done by slowly working your fingers between the breast and the skin. Work it loose to the end of the drumstick, being careful not to tear the skin.

Step 4

Using your hand, spread a generous amount of the rosemary mixture under the breast skin and down the thigh and leg. Rub the remainder of the rosemary mixture over the outside of the breast. Use toothpicks to seal skin over any exposed breast meat.

Step 5

Place the turkey on a rack in a roasting pan. Add about 1/4 inch of water to the bottom of the pan. Roast in the preheated oven 3 to 4 hours, or until the internal temperature of the bird reaches 180 degrees F (80 degrees C).

Nutrition Facts

Per Serving:

597 calories; protein 68.1g 136% DV; carbohydrates 0.8g; fat 33.7g 52% DV; cholesterol 198.3mg 66% DV; sodium 165.1mg 7% DV.

Juicy Roasted Chicken

Recipe Summary

prep:10 mins

cook:1 hr 15 mins

additional:15 mins

total:1 hr 40 mins

Servings:6

Yield:6 servings

Ingredients

1 (3 pound) whole chicken, giblets removed

salt and black pepper to taste

1 tablespoon onion powder, or to taste

½ cup margarine, divided

1 stalk celery, leaves removed

Directions

Instructions

Step 1

Preheat oven to 350 degrees F (175 degrees C).

Step 2

Place chicken in a roasting pan, and season generously inside and out with salt and pepper. Sprinkle inside and out with onion powder. Place 3 tablespoons margarine in the chicken cavity. Arrange dollops of the remaining margarine around the chicken's exterior. Cut the celery into 3 or 4 pieces, and place in the chicken cavity.

Step 3

Bake uncovered 1 hour and 15 minutes in the preheated oven, to a minimum internal temperature of 180 degrees F (82 degrees C). Remove from heat, and baste with melted margarine and drippings. Cover with aluminum foil, and allow to rest about 30 minutes before serving.

Nutrition Facts

Per Serving:

423 calories; protein 30.9g 62% DV; carbohydrates 1.2g; fat 32.1g 49% DV; cholesterol 97mg 32% DV; sodium 661.9mg 27% DV.

Simple Roasted Butternut Squash

Recipe Summary

prep:15 mins

cook:25 mins

total:40 mins

Servings: 4

Yield: 4 servings

Ingredients

1 butternut squash - peeled, seeded, and cut into 1-inch cubes

2 tablespoons olive oil

2 cloves garlic, minced

salt and ground black pepper to taste

Directions

Instructions

Step 1

Preheat oven to 400 degrees F (200 degrees C).

Step 2

Toss butternut squash with olive oil and garlic in a large bowl. Season with salt and black pepper. Arrange coated squash on a baking sheet.

Step 3

Roast in the preheated oven until squash is tender and lightly browned, 25 to 30 minutes.

Nutrition Facts

Per Serving:

177 calories; protein 2.6g 5% DV; carbohydrates 30.3g 10% DV; fat 7g 11% DV; cholesterol 0mg; sodium 10.6mg.

Roast Sticky Chicken-Rotisserie Style

Recipe Summary

prep:10 mins

cook:5 hrs

additional:4 hrs

total:9 hrs 10 mins

Servings:8

Yield:2 whole (4 pound) chickens

Ingredients

4 teaspoons salt

2 teaspoons paprika

1 teaspoon onion powder

1 teaspoon dried thyme

1 teaspoon white pepper

½ teaspoon cayenne pepper

½ teaspoon black pepper

½ teaspoon garlic powder

2 onions, quartered

2 (4 pound) whole chickens

Directions

Instructions

Step 1

In a small bowl, mix together salt, paprika, onion powder, thyme, white pepper, black pepper, cayenne pepper, and garlic powder. Remove and discard giblets from chicken. Rinse chicken cavity, and pat dry with paper towel. Rub each chicken inside and out with spice mixture. Place 1 onion into the cavity of each chicken.

Place chickens in a resealable bag or double wrap with plastic wrap. Refrigerate overnight, or at least 4 to 6 hours.

Step 2

Preheat oven to 250 degrees F (120 degrees C).

Step 3

Place chickens in a roasting pan. Bake uncovered for 5 hours, to a minimum internal temperature of 180 degrees F (85 degrees C). Let the chickens stand for 10 minutes before carving.

Nutrition Facts

Per Serving:

586 calories; protein 61.7g 124% DV; carbohydrates 3.7g 1% DV; fat 34.3g 53% DV; cholesterol 194.1mg 65% DV; sodium 1350.8mg 54% DV.

Cajun Spice Mix

Recipe Summary

prep: 5 mins

total: 5 mins

Servings: 12

Yield: 1/4 cup

Ingredients

- 2 teaspoons salt
- 2 teaspoons garlic powder
- 2 ½ teaspoons paprika
- 1 teaspoon ground black pepper
- 1 teaspoon onion powder
- 1 teaspoon cayenne pepper
- 1 ¼ teaspoons dried oregano
- 1 ¼ teaspoons dried thyme
- ½ teaspoon red pepper flakes (Optional)

Directions

Instructions

Step 1

Stir together salt, garlic powder, paprika, black pepper, onion powder, cayenne pepper, oregano, thyme, and red pepper flakes until evenly blended. Store in an airtight container.

Nutrition Facts

Per Serving:

6 calories; protein 0.2g 1% DV; carbohydrates 1.2g; fat 0.1g; cholesterol 0mg; sodium 388.2mg 16% DV.

Insalata Caprese II

Recipe Summary

prep: 15 mins

total: 15 mins

Servings: 6

Yield: 6 servings

Ingredients

4 large ripe tomatoes, sliced 1/4 inch thick

1 pound fresh mozzarella cheese, sliced 1/4 inch thick

⅓ cup fresh basil leaves

3 tablespoons extra virgin olive oil

fine sea salt to taste

freshly ground black pepper to taste

Directions

Instructions

Step 1

On a large platter, alternate and overlap the tomato slices, mozzarella cheese slices, and basil leaves. Drizzle with olive oil. Season with sea salt and pepper.

Nutrition Facts

Per Serving:

311 calories; protein 17.9g 36% DV; carbohydrates 6.6g 2% DV; fat 23.9g 37% DV; cholesterol 59.8mg 20% DV; sodium 627.3mg 25% DV.

Grilled Asparagus

Recipe Summary

prep:15 mins

cook:3 mins

total:18 mins

Servings:4

Yield:4 servings

Ingredients

1 pound fresh asparagus spears, trimmed

1 tablespoon olive oil

salt and pepper to taste

Directions

Instructions

Step 1

Preheat grill for high heat.

Step 2

Lightly coat the asparagus spears with olive oil. Season with salt and pepper to taste.

Step 3

Grill over high heat for 2 to 3 minutes, or to desired tenderness.

Nutrition Facts

Per Serving:

53 calories; protein 2.5g 5% DV; carbohydrates 4.4g 1% DV; fat 3.5g 5% DV; cholesterol 0mg; sodium 2.3mg.

Easy Herb-Roasted Turkey

Recipe Summary

prep: 15 mins

cook: 3 hrs 30 mins

additional: 30 mins

total: 4 hrs 15 mins

Servings: 16

Yield: 1 (12 pound) turkey

Ingredients

  1 (12 pound) whole turkey

  ¾ cup olive oil

  2 tablespoons garlic powder

  2 teaspoons dried basil

  1 teaspoon ground sage

  1 teaspoon salt

  ½ teaspoon black pepper

  2 cups water

Directions

Instructions

  Step 1

Preheat oven to 325 degrees F (165 degrees C). Clean turkey (discard giblets and organs), and place in a roasting pan with a lid.

Step 2

In a small bowl, combine olive oil, garlic powder, dried basil, ground sage, salt, and black pepper. Using a basting brush, apply the mixture to the outside of the uncooked turkey. Pour water into the bottom of the roasting pan, and cover.

Step 3

Bake for 3 to 3 1/2 hours, or until the internal temperature of the thickest part of the thigh measures 180 degrees F (82 degrees C). Remove bird from oven, and allow to stand for about 30 minutes before carving.

Nutrition Facts

Per Serving:

597 calories; protein 68.2g 136% DV; carbohydrates 0.9g; fat 33.7g 52% DV; cholesterol 198.3mg 66% DV; sodium 311.3mg 13% DV.

Roasted Okra

Recipe Summary

prep: 5 mins

cook: 15 mins

total: 20 mins

Servings: 3

Yield: 3 servings

Ingredients

- 18 fresh okra pods, sliced 1/3 inch thick
- 1 tablespoon olive oil
- 2 teaspoons kosher salt, or to taste
- 2 teaspoons black pepper, or to taste

Directions

Instructions

Step 1

Preheat an oven to 425 degrees F (220 degrees C).

Step 2

Arrange the okra slices in one layer on a foil lined cookie sheet. Drizzle with olive oil and sprinkle with salt and pepper. Bake in the preheated oven for 10 to 15 minutes.

Nutrition Facts

Per Serving:

65 calories; protein 1.6g 3% DV; carbohydrates 5.9g 2% DV; fat 4.6g 7% DV; cholesterol 0mg; sodium 1286.4mg 52% DV.

Pico de Gallo

Recipe Summary

prep: 20 mins

additional: 3 hrs

total: 3 hrs 20 mins

Servings: 12

Yield: 3 cups

Ingredients

- 6 roma (plum) tomatoes, diced
- ½ red onion, minced
- 3 tablespoons chopped fresh cilantro
- ½ jalapeno pepper, seeded and minced
- ½ lime, juiced
- 1 clove garlic, minced
- 1 pinch garlic powder
- 1 pinch ground cumin, or to taste
- salt and ground black pepper to taste

Directions

Instructions

Step 1

Stir the tomatoes, onion, cilantro, jalapeno pepper, lime juice, garlic, garlic powder, cumin, salt, and pepper together in a bowl. Refrigerate at least 3 hours before serving.

Nutrition Facts

Per Serving:

10 calories; protein 0.4g 1% DV; carbohydrates 2.2g 1% DV; fat 0.1g; cholesterol 0mg; sodium 15.2mg 1% DV.

Spaghetti Sauce with Ground Beef

Recipe Summary

prep: 15 mins

cook: 1 hr 10 mins

total: 1 hr 25 mins

Servings: 8

Yield: 8 servings

Ingredients

- 1 pound ground beef
- 1 onion, chopped
- 4 cloves garlic, minced

1 small green bell pepper, diced

1 (28 ounce) can diced tomatoes

1 (16 ounce) can tomato sauce

1 (6 ounce) can tomato paste

2 teaspoons dried oregano

2 teaspoons dried basil

1 teaspoon salt

½ teaspoon black pepper

Directions

Instructions

Step 1

Combine ground beef, onion, garlic, and green pepper in a large saucepan. Cook and stir until meat is brown and vegetables are tender. Drain grease.

Step 2

Stir diced tomatoes, tomato sauce, and tomato paste into the pan. Season with oregano, basil, salt, and pepper. Simmer spaghetti sauce for 1 hour, stirring occasionally.

Nutrition Facts

Per Serving:

185 calories; protein 12.4g 25% DV; carbohydrates 15g 5% DV; fat 9.3g 14% DV; cholesterol 34.8mg 12% DV; sodium 930.8mg 37% DV.

What makes Noom different?

"You can't outrun a bad diet," was the driving principle behind the project, explains Fawer. It was created by two entrepreneurs, Saeju Jeong (a serial entrepreneur from Korea) and Artem Petakov (a programmer from Ukraine who's obsessed with AI and behavior change), he says. While Petakov and Jeong felt that several existing fitness apps could be successful in helping people lose weight, they believed the root problem was much deeper- psychological.

"One of the key differences between WW and Noom is that with Noom, every user is matched with a personal health coach who's available to answer questions, provide healthful tips, and to keep you on track. You also have access to a group chat," says Batayneh. "And because motivation is a key component of behavior change, you're asked to rate your motivation on a scale of one to five."

During the process, you're set up with a personal coach who has training in the health or wellness field to act as your Noom "concierge." Coaches help users "explore what they eat and why they make the choices they do," says Fawer. "Then, we work together and consider their current habits, taste preferences, dietary restrictions, and psychological factors, to create a plan to make small, positive changes every day and develop healthier habits long term."

"A few of my clients have seen the ads and their biggest concern was that it wasn't going to be customizable enough to their lifestyle and food preferences," says Batayneh. "Many said it reminded them of WW. This also turned them off, since several have not been successful on Weight Watchers in terms of losing weight, reaching their goal, and keeping it off."

Subscribers can purchase one of two Noom memberships: the Healthy Weight Program or the Diabetes Prevention Program. The monthly rate is $59 or you can sign up annually for $199 right now (regularly $750).

CONCLUSION

Should you try the Noom diet?

"Participants in our program learn how to outsmart their own impulses, which means they're learning skills that will stick with them after they stop using Noom," says Fawer.

Noom is helpful if you want support but don't want to attend in-person meetings. And it might work pretty well for weight loss: A 2016 Scientific Reports study found that the Noom app led to weight loss in 78 percent of users across a nine-month period. However, like any new-to-the-scene diet, more scientific studies are needed before we can fully "weigh in" on the long-term results, says dietitian Bonnie Taub-Dix, R.D., creator of BetterThanDieting.com and author of Read It Before You Eat It: Taking You from Label to Table. Plus, there's nothing like in-person guidance.

"As with anything that's relatively new, it'll attract attention-but Noom users need to be motivated and willing to chart intake and activities and read related materials on their own," she says. "I'm personally not a fan of the 'good' and 'bad' finger-pointing at foods. I'm on board with the long list of fruits and veggies on their green list, but I'd hate to downplay the quality of nutrient-rich foods like nuts and seeds because they have more calories than other foods."

Regardless, any diet that takes mind and body into consideration is worth a closer look, says Taub-Dix. "The best diet is one that you can live with," she says. "Not just for a few weeks so that you can fit into a certain outfit, but for a lifetime so you can enjoy the body you're spending all of your time in!"

Made in the USA
Coppell, TX
01 April 2021